MEDICARE SIMPLIFIED

THE COMPLETE GUIDE TO UNDERSTANDING MEDICARE

ClydeBank
FINANCE

Cover Illustration and Design: Katie Poorman, Copyright © 2015 by ClydeBank Media LLC
Interior Design: Katie Poorman, Copyright © 2015 by ClydeBank Media LLC

ClydeBank Media LLC
P.O Box 6561
Albany, NY 12206
Printed in the United States of America

Copyright © 2015
ClydeBank Media LLC
www.clydebankmedia.com
All Rights Reserved

ISBN-13 : 978-0-9963667-5-5

CONTENTS

Terms displayed in *bold italic* can be found defined in the glossary on pg. 66.

INTRODUCTION

If you're reading this book seeking a confident and comprehensive understanding of Medicare to help make informed choices for yourself or for your family members, then you're going to have to be patient. *Medicare*, due to its robustness, can appear to be a lot more complicated than it actually is. As you read through this book, feel free to refer to the Glossary of Terms at the end, and be prepared to reread passages here and there when you think you may have missed something. Above all, be patient. The Medicare picture will gradually come into focus the more you study it and once you fully understand the system, you'll see that it's really not so complicated.

Medicare helps some 45 million seniors afford the costs of their increasing healthcare needs, from doctor's visits and hospital stays to durable medical equipment and prescription drugs. If you—or the Medicare *beneficiary* you seek to advise—are within three months of your 65th birthday, then it's imperative you don't delay another minute getting your feet wet with Medicare. There are key decisions to be made in the next few months. Failure to make these decisions in a timely manner could result in penalties that could affect you for the remainder of your lifetime.

We'll review the major components of Medicare and the choices available within this robust and comprehensive system. We'll also provide you with a clear road map, outlining the steps you'll need to take to get enrolled and when you need to take them. This book directs you to the very best online and offline Medicare resources to augment and supplement your reading here, while preparing you for the barrage of potentially unwanted resources that you may soon find in your mailbox if you're nearing the age of 55.

Most importantly, the goal of this book is to help you turn your Medicare entitlement into a comprehensive, cost-effective solution that will give you comfort and peace of mind as you enter the autumn years of your life.

CHAPTER ONE
How it Began & How it Has Changed

"Inadequate hospital care is an indecent penalty to place on old age," were the words of former president Lyndon B. Johnson as he spoke in May of 1964 before the Amalgamated Clothing Workers of America, a progressive labor union. A year and two months later, LBJ signed Medicare into law, guaranteeing health insurance to all Americans age 65 and older. Johnson proposed that funding for the Medicare system come from a modest contribution of earned income, which employers across the country would match. As LBJ put it in 1964: "The average manufacturing earnings in this country are now $100 a week. We ask $1 per month [from the employee] when he enters the labor market and $1 a month from his employer and the Government does not put in a single cent."

In these terms, expected Medicare contributions would constitute less than a quarter of a percent of a person's total monthly income. Not a bad trade when considering the range of *benefits* for persons approaching the autumn years of life —from prescription drugs to outpatient services to free hospital care, nursing home care, hospice care, and even certain allowances for in-home care. Today, a 2.9% payroll tax funds the program, split evenly between employee and employer, each contributing an amount equal to 1.45% of an employee's paid earnings.

Senior Health Care Before Medicare

Political libertarians are apt to remind us that senior citizens did not languish in squalor out in the streets before the advent of Medicare. Religious and charitable organizations did much to care for the nation's elders. Doctors, staying true to their Hippocratic oaths, treated patients free of charge or for very little. Hospitals rarely denied admission to an ill person who couldn't pay.

The problem with relying on the diffuse goodwill of the public was that it couldn't relieve the day-to-day stressors associated with being a senior citizen without a lot of money and without health insurance. Besides, goodwill is a great display of compassion, but it is unfortunately difficult to predict, keep consistent, or regulate.

Approximately two-thirds of senior citizens found themselves in this predicament. And even those who had insurance too often found that their policies didn't cover but a fraction of their expenses. For an uninsured or underinsured senior citizen, the prospect of getting sick or injured carried the weight of financial ruin. Seniors with small or modest savings could easily see their investments vanish in the face of mounting medical bills. There was also pressure on working families to pay out-of-pocket for the medical expenses of aged relatives.

When Medicare was first introduced, seniors paid about 19% of the costs of their healthcare. That share dipped just once and has since skyrocketed. This steep upward trend is due in part to the fact that incomes for senior citizens have changed very sluggishly as well as the dramatic increase in the cost of healthcare.

The 1972 Social Security Amendments

Medicare coverage was significantly expanded in 1972 as part of the 1972 Social Security Amendments, a massive $5 billion initiative that expanded Social Security benefits along with other entitlement programs. Medicare was made available to disabled individuals under the age of 65. Medicare was also expanded to cover dialysis and kidney transplants for individuals with end-stage renal disease.

The Balanced Budget Act of 1997

As part of a widespread effort to reign in government spending, the Balanced Budget Act of 1997 took bold measures to ensure Medicare's ongoing financial solvency. The act mandated an increase in *premium* payments for beneficiaries. It also required more careful scrutiny of Medicare payments to health care providers and health plans.

The Balanced Budget Act of 1997 gave beneficiaries the groundbreaking option to choose private health insurance plans in lieu of the standard Medicare plan. The private option, originally known as "Medicare + Choice" was revised in 2003 in the Medicare Prescription Drug, Improvement, and Modernization Act and subsequently became known as "Medicare Advantage" or MA. Medicare Advantage will be discussed in greater detail in Chapter 5 of this book.

Medicare Prescription Drug, Improvement, & Modernization Act

Signed into law by President George W. Bush in December of 2003, the Medicare Prescription Drug, Improvement, and Modernization Act updated the Medicare program to accommodate the growing importance of prescription drugs in standard health care regimens. Before the act became law, Medicare covered very few prescriptions. As part of the act's provisions, an additional benefit was set up allowing Medicare enrollees to access prescription drugs in exchange for a monthly premium payment—an out-of-pocket annual deductible and 25% *co-pays.*

Some aspects of the Medicare Prescription Drug, Improvement, and Modernization Act have been criticized as a "giveaway to drug companies," because under the law's provisions, the federal government is barred from negotiating discounts with drug companies. Additionally, the law prohibits the federal government from establishing a *formulary,* or listing of which drugs can be prescribed under various insurance plans. The law does not prevent private health care providers from establishing formularies.

Desegregation Through Medicare

When the Medicare bill was signed into law, the issue of racial segregation, especially in the South, was still front and center in the public consciousness. In 1966, the Johnson administration leveraged the new Medicare law in an interesting tactic aimed at hastening desegregation. In order to be eligible to receive payments from Medicare, hospitals were required to desegregate their facilities.

CHAPTER TWO

Getting Enrolled

In the world of Medicare, age 65 is the year to act. Unlike Social Security, there's no incentive to defer Medicare enrollment past the age of 65. Currently, some Social Security beneficiaries may elect to start receiving their benefits before or after their full retirement age—currently 67—though at a penalty. If you are planning for retirement, or have questions regarding the complexities and nuances of the Social Security system, pick up a copy of *Social Security Simplified* by ClydeBank Finance. Within its pages you'll learn the ins and outs of the Social Security system along with the best ways to maximize your benefit.

In fact, much the opposite of Social Security, if you delay enrolling in Medicare you may be subject to an increase in your monthly Part B premiums after you enroll. As of now, seniors pay a little over $100 a month for Medicare Part B ($104.90 a month in 2015). However, this monthly premium increases by 10% if you delay enrollment for a year. It goes up by 20% if you delay enrollment for two years, and it climbs an additional 10% for every year that you delay enrollment.

Medicare Part B covers outpatient care. Part B is the only Medicare component that requires beneficiaries to pay a monthly premium. A breakdown of Medicare parts A-D will be featured in Chapter 3.

The specific window for Part B enrollment spans seven months, centered on the month of your 65th

-4 mo.	-3 mo.	-2 mo.	-1 mo.	(65)	+1 mo.	+2 mo.	+3 mo.	+4 mo.
Too Soon to Enroll	*Enrollment window – 3 months before your* *65th birthday to 3 months after*							Penalties Begin

Fg.1 : The specific window for Part B enrollment is seven months long. It opens three months before the month in which you turn 65 and closes three months after that month.

birthday. You may enroll three months before or three months after that date before penalties are levied on your Part B premium. If your birthday is on the first day of the month, then your Part B coverage starts the first day of the month prior, otherwise it starts on the first day of your birthday month.

Penalties are not levied on your Part B premium if you're still working at age 65 and are covered by your employer's group health insurance plan. Nor are penalties levied if you're covered under your spouse's employer's group health insurance. You will be subject to a 'special enrollment period' after you or your spouse retires.

If a retiree's birthday is May 16th, on that person's 65th birthday he or she may enroll as early as February, March, or April. If that person waits to enroll until after the month of May, then enrollment may be made penalty-free through June, July, and at the latest, August. After August penalties, begin to accrue.

Important! – If you're going to remain on your employer's (or your spouse's employer's) group plan past your 65th birthday, then you need to ascertain whether the employer's insurance is going to be 'primary' or 'secondary' in relation to Medicare. This is where people often get into trouble.

If the employer's insurance is secondary to Medicare (as is common in smaller companies with 20 or fewer employees), then you need to enroll in Medicare at age 65, even if you are still covered by your or your spouse's employer group plan. If an insurance plan is secondary to Medicare, then it will pay a small percentage of a *claim* (usually 20%) only after the primary insurer, Medicare, pays for the bulk of the initial claim.

Employers with more than 20 employees usually have insurance plans that are deemed primary in relation to Medicare. These plans will pay for the bulk of your medical bills, even if you're 65 or older, without Medicare Part B. If the employer's plan is a primary plan and you're satisfied with the coverage, then you can probably get by without enrolling in Medicare Part B. You'll be eligible for the special enrollment period after you or your spouse retires, so you will avoid penalties. Nonetheless, you may still be in a better financial position if you enroll in Medicare Part B. To make this determination, you should evaluate the types of claims you're likely to submit, figure out how much your employer's insurance (primary insurance) will cover, and figure out how much additional coverage will be available to you if you take the extra step and enroll in Medicare.

You may find that paying the Medicare Part B monthly premium is worth it, given the amount of out-of-pocket expenses you'll save. Your or your spouse's employer's HR department should be able to provide you with coverage details that specify how that employer's plan and Medicare interact.

In some instances, employer plans will automatically convert into Medicare private plans (also known as Medicare Part C or Medicare Plus) once the employee turns 65.

You may also decide that you're better off enrolling in Medicare and electing to use it as your primary insurer in lieu of your employer's group plan.

Even if your employer's group plan will act as your primary insurance and you're going to wait to enroll in Medicare Part B, you should still enroll in Medicare Part A at age 65, as there is no premium and you will get additional coverage for hospital care.

Former Employees Who Are Covered Under Retiree Plans

If you're 65, not working, and have health insurance through your former employer's retiree plan, then you should still enroll in Medicare. Retiree plans almost always assume the role of 'secondary' plans after age 65. You will need Medicare to pay for the bulk of your health care expenses. Seniors who are already enrolled to receive Social Security benefits at age 65 will be automatically enrolled in Medicare. These seniors will receive their Medicare cards automatically in the mail about three months before their 65th birthdays.

If you are not receiving Social Security, then you'll fare best if you apply for Medicare about three months before your 65th birthday. You can apply at your local Social Security Administration office or online at _www.ssa.gov/medicareonly._

Surcharges for Higher-Income Seniors

If you're earning more than $85,000 in annual income, then you will be subject to a Medicare surcharge. For joint filers, the cap is $170,000 in annual income. The surcharges will not only be applied to Medicare Part B, but also to Medicare Advantage (Part C) and the prescription drug benefit (Part D). The amount of the surcharge is significant and rises through four income brackets. Seniors in the first surcharge bracket pay an additional $480 just for Part B.

Assistance for Lower-Income Seniors

Lower-income seniors may find that even the $104.90/monthly premium is a stretch for their budgets. These seniors may qualify for a Medicare Savings Program (MSP), which is a type of state-based financial aid for low-income Medicare beneficiaries. You can get more information about this and apply for an MSP at your state Medicaid office.

MSP programs come in four flavors :
- Qualified Medicare Beneficiary (QMB) Program
- Specified Low-Income Medicare Beneficiaries (SLMB) Program
- Qualified Individual (QI) Program
- Qualified Disabled and Working Individuals (QDWI) Program

The Various MSP Programs		
QMB	Low-income beneficiaries may qualify.	Helps cover a portion of Part A and Part B premiums.	Covers a portion of Medicare deductibles
SLMB	This program pays the Part B premiums for those who qualify for QMB but have excess income that would otherwise disqualify them.		
QI	This is a temporary program that pays for the Part B premiums for qualifying individuals.	To qualify, beneficiaries must only make between 120 and 135 percent of the federal poverty level.	
QDWI	This program allows individuals who became eligible for Medicare due to receipt of Social Security disability insurance (SSDI) to continue to receive Medicare coverage while attempting to go back to work.	This program still applies even if, while working, an individual makes too much money to continue receiving SS benefits.	

13

When to Delay Drug Coverage (Part D)

If your employer plan is providing good coverage for your prescription drug costs, then you need not sign up for Medicare Part D right away. Check with your employer and ask if the drug plan meets Medicare's definition of a 'creditable' plan. If the plan is creditable, then you can wait until you no longer have it before enrolling in Medicare Part D.

Enrollment Periods Defined

Your Initial Enrollment Period (IEP) for Medicare is usually a seven month window, beginning about 100 days before you turn 65 and ending 100 days afterward. Enrolling during your IEP will ensure that you do not incur penalties on your Part B premium. If you miss your IEP, then you can enroll any year during the General Enrollment Period (GEP) from January 1st through March 31st every year.

Get Ready to be Solicited

Many consumers may be aware of the 'Do Not Call' list—the FCC's registry of over 200 million Americans who would prefer not to receive telemarketing calls—but just recently in 2015, the Federal Communications Commission has further strengthened already robust consumer protection laws with the addition of even more protections to the 1991 Telephone Consumer Protection Act (TCPA).

Part C of Medicare, known as Medicare Advantage, allows private insurers to contract with Medicare and administer services. Never ones to turn down a paying customer, private insurers devise and market specialized Medicare plans and would like nothing better than for you to choose their plans over their competitors. As a result, you should brace yourself, because if you've just turned or are about to turn 65, then you're going to be the target of some major marketing efforts.

Don't worry; you shouldn't get any calls at your house. To solve the problem of aggressive marketing agents, the CMS (Center for Medicare and Medicaid Services) conducted a lengthy investigation and put some specific rules in place to limit the intrusiveness of Medicare Advantage marketing.

Among these rules:

- **No calls or unsolicited visits to your home are permitted.** Agents may only call you if you are already signed up for a plan.

- **No agent is permitted to try and steer you into a specific plan.** While it is a sales person's job to sell, they are prohibited from manipulating the sale of insurance as a component of Part C Medicare.

- **An agent must never state or imply that you are going to lose your Medicare coverage unless you choose a specific plan or Medicare Advantage provider.** Not only would such a misleading statement subordinate your best interests, it would also be untrue.

- **An agent must never offer you cash or gifts of any kind in exchange for signing up for a specific health care plan.** Many forms of insurance in many states do not allow rebating or giving/receiving gifts in exchange for insurance. This extends to life insurance, home or auto insurance, and others, though these types of insurance are regulated at the state, not federal level.

- **An agent must not attempt to enroll you in a plan over the phone** unless you made the initial phone call to the agent and specifically asked him to enroll you.

- **Agents must not attempt to sell you any products other than the ones in which you specifically stated your interest when you set up the appointment.** It's the agent's responsibility to either record your initial phone call or document your conversation in writing to verify the products you originally agreed to discuss.

A Medicare Advantage marketing representative has a financial incentive to get you to enroll for coverage with the insurer that he or she represents. Some of these financial incentives, at one point in time, were so exorbitant that the CMS had to lay out some restrictions on how much commission these marketing representatives could earn. The CMS now strives to ensure that Medicare Advantage marketing representatives are knowledgeable, licensed, and more focused on education than selling.

Some marketers and agents are only interested in speaking with you after you turn 65, in hopes that they can compel you to enroll in a Medicare Advantage plan immediately. Others will sit down and talk with you before you turn 65. If you want to be educated rather than pitched, you're better off meeting with agents prior to turning 65.

As you approach your 65th birthday, you'll begin to receive a multitude of Medicare mailers from private insurers such as Blue Shield, United Health Care, Humana, and Kaiser Permanente. Some of these mailers will include thick books, and you may not know where to begin. From the table of contents, try to locate the Summary of Benefits for each insurance provider and focus on the types of services, equipment, and prescription drugs that you anticipate using. Compare the premiums, co-pays, and deductibles for the various plans.

The physician networks will usually be the same from carrier to carrier—these are the physicians who have agreed to accept payment from Medicare Advantage. The sole exception will be Kaiser Permanente, which uses its own private network of physicians and pharmacies.

You may determine that you'd rather just stick with Medicare itself as your health benefits administrator. The AARP calls this decision—to sick with *Original Medicare* or to choose a Medicare Advantage plan—the most paramount decision you'll make as a new Medicare beneficiary. In Chapter 5, we'll review in-depth key comparison points between original Medicare and Medicare Advantage plans.

Enrolling in Medigap

In addition to Medicare Advantage (Part C) offerings, Medicare beneficiaries may also turn to Medigap for supplemental coverage. Supplemental coverage means that you'll pay a higher monthly premium but will have extra help with out-of-pocket expenses, such as deductibles and co-pays. Note that the terms Medigap and supplemental coverage are interchangeable.

Right after you enroll in Medicare Part B, you will have a *one-time* window to enroll in any Medigap coverage policy in your state that lasts for six months starting from your 65th birthday and when you became enrolled in Medicare Part B. Your current health condition in no way limits your choices during this enrollment period. If you miss this enrollment period, however, it's possible that you could be denied for certain Medigap plans or that you could be asked to pay higher premiums.

Take a look at the following list of things to know about Medigap:

- You must have Medicare Part A and Part B to enroll in any Medigap supplemental plans.

- The monthly premium that you pay to your private insurer is separate from (and in addition to) your monthly Part B premium.

- Couples seeking enrollment in Medigap policies need to purchase their own individual policies; a *Medigap policy* only covers a single person.

- Medigap policies sold after January 1, 2006 aren't allowed to include coverage for prescription drugs. Beneficiaries must turn to a Part D plan for their drug coverage.

Many people turn to Medigap or supplemental coverage if they are concerned with the quality of healthcare they will receive. While traditional Medicare is a far-reaching policy with so many participating doctors that many people don't struggle to find a healthcare professional that fits their needs, some retirees stress the need to be able to find an expert doctor *anywhere* in the country. A supplemental plan significantly increases your choices when selecting your doctor, but remember the associated costs in the form of higher premiums and other, possibly less obvious costs.

What are some of the *out-of-pocket costs* that Medigap strives to reduce? Blood, for one thing. Interestingly enough, patients on Medicare pay for the first three pints of blood for a transfusion. Another oddity that isn't covered is foreign emergency care. While these aren't necessarily reasons in themselves to purchase a supplemental plan, they do demonstrate that there are a lot of circumstances in which Medicare is not as robust as some retirees would have hoped.

Of course there are surprises too. Medicare may cover some weight loss surgery. Known as bariatric surgery, your procedure may qualify for coverage if you have a Body Mass Index (BMI) of 35 or higher and you have serious health conditions relating to weight.

In the following chapters, you'll get an idea of what's covered under Medicare and what's not, and you will better understand what additional coverage, if any, you will require. We'll look at each of the lettered parts in greater detail and discuss how you can make Medicare work best for your situation.

CHAPTER THREE
Medicare Benefits – Part A : Hospital Care

Medicare benefits are divided into four parts—A, B, C and D—and these component parts are referenced frequently in most any discussion or writing on the subject. If you don't already, it's important to have at least a basic understanding of what each part entails.

The four parts of Medicare are:
- *Medicare Part A : Hospital Insurance*
- *Medicare Part B : Medical Insurance*
- *Medicare Part C : Medicare Advantage*
- *Medicare Part D : Prescription Drug Coverage*

Let's review each part in more detail, beginning with:

Medicare Part A : Hospital Insurance

If a beneficiary is covered by Medicare Part A, then there should be text reading "Hospital Part A" in the bottom left corner of the beneficiary's red, white, and blue Medicare card.

Medicare Part A covers inpatient expenses, such as hospital stays. In this capacity, Part A payments help to cover the first 90 days of inpatient hospital care. The first 60 days are covered nearly in full, requiring only a one-time deductible payment of $1,216. Beginning on day 61 and following through day 90, a co-pay of $315 is required for each hospital day. If a Medicare beneficiary requires more than 90 days of hospital care within a given **benefit period**, then the beneficiary may draw from a pool of 60 **lifetime reserve days**. The co-pay required per lifetime reserve day used is $630.

19

For the purpose of Medicare Part A, new 'benefit periods' begin once the beneficiary has gone for 60 days without receiving any hospital care. Once a new benefit period begins, benefits essentially renew in full. Beneficiaries are again eligible to pay their $1,216 deductibles and receive 60 days of hospital care. Lifetime reserve days, however, do not renew with a new benefit period.

Medicare will not pay for private-duty nursing, nor will it pay for a private hospital room unless it's necessary given the patient's condition. If the hospital charges extra for television and phone access, Medicare will not foot these bills.

First 60 Days	Days 61 – 90	90+ Days
One-time deductible payment of $1,216	Co-pay of $315 for each hospital day	Co-pay of $630 is needed per lifetime reserve day used

Fg.2 : A chart demonstrating the costs of inpatient care under Medicare Part A. It is important to note that this structure resets for every new benefits period. A new benefits period begins when a beneficiary has gone 60 days without receiving any hospital care. While the first 90 days of extended hospital stay reset, a beneficiary's lifetime reserve does not.

Medicare Part A will also pay for care received at a skilled nursing facility (SNF) when certain conditions are met. Skilled nursing care involves specialized medical attentions such as therapies—physical or speech therapy, for example—or administering intravenous injections. Skilled nursing facilities may be located in hospitals or integrated into assisted living centers.

In order for Medicare to cover SNF care, the following conditions must all be true:

- The beneficiary must have days available to use in his or her benefit period. If the beneficiary has used all 90 days in a given period for hospital care, then he or she will not be eligible to receive Medicare coverage for SNF care until the next benefit period begins (60 days without hospital care).

- The beneficiary must have been in the hospital for three days. The day he or she enters the hospital is considered day number one, but the day the beneficiary leaves the hospital is not included. This period is known as a 'qualifying hospital stay'.

- Generally, if a beneficiary has been receiving skilled nursing care then returns home for a period of time before again returning to an SNF facility, he or she need not go back to the hospital for three days in order for Medicare to cover subsequent periods of SNF care. To qualify, the beneficiary's doctor must have ordered the SNF care.

- The skilled care service being administered must be required on a daily basis. Patients receiving therapy, which often include full rest days, are still said to be receiving 'daily care', even if they are only technically receiving services five or six days out of the week.

- The condition for which the beneficiary is receiving skilled care must be a condition for which he or she was treated during the three-day qualifying hospital stay.

- The skilled services must be an appropriate and necessary response to the condition for which the beneficiary is being treated.

- The skilled services must be administered in a Medicare-certified SNF.

Benefit periods for skilled nursing care run for 100 days and are renewed when the beneficiary has neither been in an SNF nor a hospital for 60 consecutive days or longer. If the beneficiary has continued to reside in an SNF without receiving any skilled care there for 60 consecutive days or longer, then the benefit period may renew. There is no limit to the number of benefit periods available to a Medicare beneficiary over the course of a lifetime; however, when skilled care coverage is sought at the beginning of any new benefit period, the beneficiary must first check back into the hospital and establish another three-day qualifying hospital stay.

The rules get confusing when a beneficiary stops receiving skilled care for 30 days but resumes care within the following 30 days. If the beneficiary stops receiving skilled care for at least 30 days but fewer than 60 days, his SNF benefit period will not renew, but the beneficiary will still require a three-day qualifying hospital stay before resuming skilled care.

Consider the following example: John has received 15 days of physical therapy for a sciatic nerve injury. The pain subsides, so John goes home on day 16. Fifteen days later (day 31) the pain comes back and feels just as fierce as ever. John's benefit period has not yet renewed, so Medicare will only cover an additional 85 days of skilled care, and since John has not received skilled care for at least 30 days, he must first go back to the hospital to establish a new three-day qualifying hospital stay.

Had John's pain come back only two days earlier (day 29), then he would have been able to return directly to the skilled nursing care facility and would not have had to first return to the hospital. Had John's pain returned on day 60 or afterwards, then his benefit period would have fully renewed, meaning that he'd have to do his 3 days at the hospital, but would then have a full 100 days of SNF coverage at his disposal. Simply put, if a patient is receiving SNF care, temporarily stops receiving care and then resumes it:

Ceasing then Resuming SNF Care under Medicare Part A		
Within 30 Days	The beneficiary need not return to the hospital before resuming SNF care.	The benefit period will not renew, as the beneficiary has not gone 60 consecutive days without SNF or hospital care.
Within 60 Days but after at least 30 Days	The beneficiary must first return to the hospital for three days before resuming SNF care.	The benefit period will not renew.
After 60 Days have passed	The beneficiary must first return to the hospital for three days before resuming SNF care.	The benefit period will renew assuming the beneficiary has not been in the hospital or obtained any other SNF care within the last 60 days.

Does Medicare Part A Pay for Nursing Home or Assisted Living Expenses?

While Medicare will pay for skilled nursing care for periods of limited duration, it will not pay for custodial care services. Custodial care refers to common nursing home or assisted living services that are set up to assist people with basic aspects of day-to-day living, such as bathing, cooking, using the bathroom, and getting out of bed. For low-income individuals in need of support with custodial care at a nursing home or assisted living facility, *Medicaid*, not Medicare, is the appropriate resource.

Does Medicare Part A Pay for Hospice Care?

Hospice care refers to the care strategy adopted once a patient has been deemed to be terminally ill. Rather than focus on treating and curing the disease, hospice care is intended to maximize the patient's comfort. Hospice care is multi-faceted and includes clinical, pharmacological, mental and spiritual support. Hospice care is typically administered at the home of the terminally ill patient. For Medicare beneficiaries who—with the counsel of their physicians—decide to pursue hospice care, certain benefits are available.

- **Medicare provides hospice care to its beneficiaries essentially free of charge.** No initial co-payments or deductible payments are required.

- **Beneficiaries may be required to pay $5 co-pays for prescription drugs and other products used to facilitate pain relief during in-home hospice care.** Most if not all hospice-related drugs are covered under Medicare Part A if their purpose is to alleviate pain and control other symptoms for the patient. Drugs are not covered if their purpose is to cure illness, which is not the intent of hospice care. Beneficiaries, with the counsel of their physicians, will be asked to sign a statement declaring their intent to pursue only hospice care.

- **Medicare will pay for most respite care services.** *Respite care* refers to the temporary lodging of a patient receiving hospice care in a hospital or other facility so that the family member or friend taking care of the beneficiary at home may take some time away. The beneficiary may be responsible for paying 5% of respite care expenses.

To get a detailed breakdown of the out-of-pocket expenses that will be incurred during hospice care, the best course of action is to talk to your physician or health care provider. He or she will be able to assess other factors such as whether you have additional insurance beyond Medicare such as life insurance. Your health care provider will also assess local factors such as how much the hospice doctor charges and the cost of various services in your region.

Once a beneficiary chooses to receive hospice care, Medicare will not cover any expenses for treatments aimed at curing the terminal illness, nor will it pay for ambulance transportation or emergency room visits unless they result from separate events unrelated to the terminal illness, such as a fall. Medicare will not pay for the beneficiary's room and board during hospice care, neither at the beneficiary's own home nor at a nursing home.

Will Medicare pay for Home Health Services?

When certain conditions are met, Medicare Part A will cover in-home care, such as physical therapy, speech-language pathology, and continued occupational therapy. In order for Medicare to foot the bill for these services, the patient's doctor must certify that one of the aforementioned services is necessary.

In order for Medicare to cover home health care services, the services must be complex enough to warrant the involvement of a professional. The physician who orders the home health care must believe that the condition can be improved within a reasonable and predictable amount of time. The home health agency assigned to administer the services must be Medicare-certified. Finally, in order for Medicare to pay for home health services, the patient must be deemed 'homebound', meaning that it is ill-advised for him to leave his home because of the risk or the required expenditure of effort. Homebound individuals often have mobility issues, requiring the use of wheelchairs, canes, or crutches. Keep in mind that individuals can still be deemed 'homebound' even if they leave their homes infrequently for limited periods of time to receive medical services or to attend religious services.

Medicare does not cover 24-hour home care, personal care or services like meal deliveries, laundry, or home cleaning. If a patient receives home care through Medicare, then the services being rendered must be skilled services intended to treat a specific medical condition. Patients do not pay any co-payment or deductible for home health care services but are required to pay 20% of the **Medicare approved amount** of medical equipment such as crutches, walkers, or physical therapy aides.

As a best practice, Medicare beneficiaries seeking home health care services should contact the home health service provider to ascertain what services and equipment Medicare covers and what, if any, they will have to pay for out-of-pocket. In order to protect beneficiaries from unknowingly receiving services or supplies not covered by Medicare, home health care providers are required to provide their patients with a 'Home Health Advance Beneficiary Notice', which clarifies what services are and aren't covered under Medicare.

'Medicare approved amount' refers to the negotiated amount of money that Medicare is willing to pay for various services. When doctors or other health care service providers agree to take payments from Medicare, they agree to a defined payment schedule for products and services. For example, a doctor may ordinarily charge $300 to put a cast on a broken leg, but if he or she wants to treat patients using Medicare, then that doctor must agree to bill only the Medicare approved amount for that particular service, which is often less—if not significantly less—than what the doctor would normally charge.

What are Quality Improvement Organizations?

Quality Improvement Organizations (QIOs) are groups of doctors and other health care professionals who provide feedback to the federal government in order to review the care given to Medicare patients. QIOs are broken into each of the states and focus on the care administered there.

QIOs are relevant to patients in a number of ways. First and foremost they are the authority when it comes to care. They determine not only if a procedure, consultation, or other form of care is medically necessary, but whether or not it is delivered in the most appropriate setting. These two overarching characteristics of any given care scenario are the baseline indicators of whether a procedure or care will be covered by Medicare.

Quality Improvement Organizations also respond to and investigate patient complaints concerning the quality of care. This means reviewing notices of non-coverage issued to beneficiaries from hospitals upon request. There can be some confusion on the part of the patient who may not be medically literate as to whether a specific case is actually covered by Medicare or not. The inverse is also true. Physicians may make poor judgment calls concerning the eligibility of a procedure, treatment, or care, and when patients contest this, the QIOs must investigate and make a ruling.

When a patient is admitted to a Medicare-participating hospital, the patient is given a statement entitled *An Important Message from Medicare* that outlines not only the patient's rights, but also the contact information for the QIO of that state for the submission of appeals and requests of review.

CHAPTER FOUR

Medicare Benefits – Part B : Medical Care

The four parts of Medicare are:

- *Medicare Part A : Hospital Insurance*
- *Medicare Part B : Medical Insurance*
- *Medicare Part C : Medicare Advantage*
- *Medicare Part D : Prescription Drug Coverage*

Let's review the next part in more detail:

Medicare Part B : Medical Insurance

The majority of Medicare benefits fall under Medicare Part B: Medical Insurance. If a beneficiary has Medicare Part B coverage, "Medical (Part B)" appears on the bottom left corner of his or her red, white and blue Medicare card. Medicare Part B includes visits to the doctor, diagnosis and treatment, ambulance transportation, and outpatient hospital services such as lab tests and surgeries. Medicare Part B also covers supplies deemed to be medically necessary for a patient's treatment and medications administered by a physician during a visit. When Medicare was first introduced, the larger share of spending—by about two-thirds—was what is now called Part A or inpatient care. Since then there has been a significant shift, and Part B now accounts for the majority of all Medicare spending.

Other medical procedures covered by Medicare Part B include but aren't limited to:

- Blood transfusions
- Immunosuppressive drugs used for organ transplants
- Renal dialysis chemotherapy
- Hormonal treatments
- Flu shots

Durable medical equipment covered by Medicare Part B includes but isn't limited to:

- Oxygen tents
- Iron lungs
- Walking canes
- CPAP
- Hospital beds
- Wheelchairs
- Catheters
- Nebulizers
- Blood sugar monitors

> Durable medical equipment, also known as DME, refers to long-lasting medical equipment recommended by a doctor for in-home medical use. Medicare will only cover DME expenses if both the doctors and DME suppliers are enrolled in Medicare. To be enrolled, Medicare subjects both doctors and suppliers to strict standards. Always ask whether a doctor or supplier participates in Medicare before taking any DME.

Part B Premiums, Deductibles & Co-pays

Medicare Part B is most commonly used for visits to the doctor and basic outpatient medical services. For services that require co-pays, 20% is the standard amount. Annual deductibles for Part B services are close to $150. As explained in Chapter 2 of this book, the beneficiary's income affects the premiums for Part B. As of 2015, the baseline premium for original Medicare Part B is $104.90.

Preventive Care

Part B covers preventive health services free of charge during your first 12 months of enrollment and offers annual wellness check-ups every year afterward. Preventive care includes physicals and, per the provisions of the Affordable Care Act, now includes bone mass measurements and breast cancer screenings. In order to get guaranteed free preventive care, you will have to be sure to obtain your services from a provider who accepts *assignment*.

Assignment is a very important term in Medicare. It refers to whether or not a physician who accepts Medicare patients has agreed to pay the Medicare Approved Amount for services.

> **For example**, let's say patient X has a broken wrist and visits physician Y, who normally charges $250 to reset and put a cast on a broken wrist. Let's say that the Medicare Approved Amount for treating a broken wrist is $200, and physician Y is a doctor who accepts assignment. This means that physician Y has agreed to pay the Medicare Approved Amount for services when treating Medicare patients. Physician Y will bill Medicare $160 for the procedure (80%) and patient X will pay a $40 co-pay (20%).

> Now, let's consider a similar situation in which, instead of visiting physician Y, patient X visits physician Z, who also charges $250 dollars to treat a broken wrist but does not take assignment. Physicians like physician Z can still see Medicare patients, but they are not limited to charging only the Medicare Approved Amount for their services. Nonetheless, these physicians are still restricted by another Medicare rule called 'the limiting charge'.

> The limiting charge rule holds that any physician treating a Medicare patient is not permitted to charge more than 115% of the Medicare Approved Amount. So, if physician Z treated patient X for his broken wrist, and the Medicare Approved Amount for the procedure is $200, then the most that physician Z could charge would be $230, or 115% of $200. Patient X would again pay 20% ($46), and Medicare would pay the remaining 80% ($184).

Welcome to Medicare Visit

As part of Medicare's preventive care coverage, all patients who have coverage under Part B are eligible to receive a 'Welcome to Medicare' preventive visit. During this visit, the beneficiary's physician records some basic observations and takes some basic measurements. The physician reviews the beneficiary's medical history and makes him or her aware of the types of illnesses to which he or she is vulnerable due to genetics or other factors. The physician also reviews the beneficiary's risk factors for depression.

Also included in Part B coverage, and new per the mandates of the Affordable Care Act, is the Annual Wellness Visit. This is an opportunity for the beneficiary to meet with his or her physician once a year for the purpose of discussing preventive care. The discussion may focus on productive lifestyle choices or any new mental health concerns that may have developed since the initial Welcome visit.

During the beneficiary's first Wellness visit, he or she will fill out a questionnaire called a 'Health Risk Assessment' that will allow the physician to produce a personalized prevention plan. The physician will also compile a list of all the other health care providers that the beneficiary currently accesses on a regular basis and all the prescriptions she currently uses. Medical and family history will also be discussed and updated as needed. Mental health vulnerabilities will be reviewed with the beneficiary along with preventive measures. Finally, a basic assessment will be made of the beneficiary's ability to perform regular day-to-day functions safely and effectively, paying special attention to risk of falling, safety in the home, and hearing impairment.

For subsequent Annual Wellness visits, the beneficiary's medical and family history factors will be revised, and the patient will receive renewed and revised counsel from the physician on preventive care.

During an Annual Wellness visit, the physician may refer the patient to health education or preventive care services such as those designed to reduce risk of falling, improve nutrition, and improve physical activity. Programs are also available to help Medicare beneficiaries stop smoking and lose weight as needed, wanted, or recommended.

As part of the preventive care regimen, physicians will likely order one or multiple preventive tests and screenings in response to the beneficiary's unique health risk factors.

These tests and screenings may include but are not limited to:

- Alcohol dependency/abuse screening & counseling
- Colorectal cancer screening
- Diabetes screening
- Glaucoma screening
- Hepatitis C screening
- Prostate cancer screening
- Mammograms
- Pap tests

There are no co-pays required for either the Welcome to Medicare visit or the initial or subsequent Annual Wellness visits. The expense of these visits also does not count towards the beneficiary's Part B (or any) deductible.

Mental Health Coverage Under Part B

All mental health related issues requiring inpatient services, such as hospitalization or assignment to a psychiatric facility, are covered per the dictates of Medicare Part A and adhere to the same co-pays, deductibles, and benefit period timelines described in Chapter 3 of this book. For outpatient mental health services, such as counseling, coverage is provided through Medicare Part B and, generally, the same deductible and 20% co-pay (20% of the Medicare approved amount) applies for mental health services.

> If mental health outpatient services are administered in a hospital, the beneficiary may be subject to a slightly higher co-pay. This co-pay amount will vary but can be as high as 40% of the Medicare approved amount.

The beneficiary's primary care physician is required to offer one free depression screening every year. This will be administered without collecting any co-pay from the beneficiary.

Depending on the severity of the beneficiary's mental health condition, a treatment plan may be recommended that isn't completely covered under Medicare. This scenario usually results when the primary physician thinks the patient would best benefit from a frequency or type of treatment that's beyond the standard reach of Medicare coverage, such as marriage counseling or geriatric daycare. Talk to your health care provider to help clarify any questions you have about what is or isn't covered under Medicare.

Services that are covered by Medicare include but are not limited to:
- Individual and group psychotherapy
- Psychiatric evaluation
- Medication management
- Family counseling (so long as treatment of the beneficiary is the primary focus)
- Diagnostic tests
- Prescription drugs that can't be self-administered

Using Medicare to Get a Second Opinion

Believe it or not, when a physician recommends a particularly intrusive, dangerous, or expensive procedure such as a surgery, he often encourages his patients to seek a second opinion. The idea is that even doctors make mistakes; a second opinion could catch an aspect of the diagnosis that your physician may have missed. Think of it as the medical equivalent of the old carpenter's saying "measure twice, cut once." Medicare Part B coverage provides coverage to beneficiaries who need to acquire second opinions before undergoing major procedures, so long as a Medicare physician provides the opinion.

To get a qualified second opinion, find a physician who takes Medicare and has expertise in the area of concern, and schedule an appointment. The beneficiary should have the primary physician's office send the beneficiary's complete medical history over to the office of the new physician. If the new physician disagrees with the assessment of the primary physician, then the beneficiary may either make his own decision on whose advice to take, pursue the opinion of a third Medicare physician, or return to the primary physician to discuss the issue further.

CHAPTER FIVE

Medicare Benefits – Part C : Medicare Advantage

The four parts of Medicare are:
- *Medicare Part A : Hospital Insurance*
- *Medicare Part B : Medical Insurance*
- *Medicare Part C : Medicare Advantage*
- *Medicare Part D : Prescription Drug Coverage*

Let's review the next part in more detail:

Medicare Part C : Medicare Advantage

With Medicare Part C, also known as Medicare Advantage, beneficiaries can choose to have their Medicare Part A and Part B (also known as original Medicare) administered and customized by a private insurer, usually a Health Maintenance Organization (HMO) or Preferred Provider Organization (PPO).

Private insurers are offered a certain amount of funding from Medicare that they can incorporate into the design of a competitive health insurance product that offers *all the benefits* of Part A and Part B, while usually offering expanded benefits such as hearing, vision, or dental. Some Part C plans also limit the amount of out-of-pocket expenses that a Medicare beneficiary can incur. For example, a Part C plan can eliminate all co-pays after a total amount of $1,500 in co-pays has been paid out for the year. These types of perks, however, will also usually come with higher monthly premiums. Medicare Part C beneficiaries are still technically on the hook for their standard income-based Part B monthly premiums ($104.90 per month is the most common Part B premium amount), but the Part C plan may cover all or part of the Part

B premium on behalf of the beneficiary.

The enrollment period for Medicare Advantage is different from that of original Medicare. Beneficiaries who decide to enroll in Medicare Advantage must do so during 'open enrollment', which is between October 15th and December 7th.

Medicare Part C vs. Original Medicare

Every Medicare beneficiary must decide whether to go with a Part C plan or stick with the original Medicare. Here are some factors to consider:

Your Network of Providers

Original Medicare will incorporate all providers that take Medicare, while the Part C/Advantage providers are going to limit their networks to only those who take Blue Shield, Humana, United Health Care or whatever private insurer is administering the Part C plan.

The patient will generally have fewer options for providers with Part C. Part C plans are also likely to restrict the physician network regionally, which can make getting health care services while traveling difficult. For this reason, a lot of retirees who like to roam about the country tend to stick with original Medicare. Limited physician networks create a serious disadvantage to seniors that live in rural areas as well. Many rural physicians are simply not 'in network,' and lengthy travel times can prove costly. This cost is even more pronounced if the retiree in question suffers from a chronic condition.

Going to See Specialists

Medicare Advantage plans are generally HMOs or PPOs; getting to a specialist may require first going to the primary care provider (PHP)—the patient's general doctor—before being permitted to go see a specialist. PPOs do allow patients to go directly to a specialist so long as the specialist is part of the PPO's network. If the patient wants to circumvent this system, going outside of the network will cost a lot more.

In original Medicare, beneficiaries are allowed to go directly to specialists without having to obtain referrals from their PHPs.

Premiums & Other Expenses

Premiums are either the same or higher with Medicare Advantage plans, but the out-of-pocket expenses are often reigned in. When comparing expected costs, write out a yearlong medical forecast for yourself. How often will you be visiting a doctor, and what types of tests or procedures do you expect to have done? What will your out-of-pocket expenses look like with varying plans? Chart your projected expenses with original Medicare, and then chart them with a couple of Medicare Advantage plans that look attractive to you.

To aid you in your initial estimates, here are some statistics on Medicare patients compiled by the Kaiser Foundation. In 2006:

- Eight out of 10 Medicare beneficiaries saw a doctor. The median number of visits was 6.
- One out of 5 Medicare beneficiaries was hospitalized over the course of the year.
- Premiums for Medicare C plans were, on average, $30 a month for HMOs and $32 to $60 for PPOs. These premiums were in addition to the standard Medicare Part B premium.
- Three out of 10 beneficiaries visited the emergency room on at least one occasion.
- Eight percent of Medicare beneficiaries used home health services, with a median of 17 home health service visits in the year.

Employer Coverage

If you're receiving health care coverage from your current or former employer, then review the section in Chapter 2 of this book regarding the interactions between various Medicare plans and employer coverage. Definitive facts on the matter should be obtainable through your company's HR department or through the Social Security Administration.

Additionally, religious fraternal benefit society plans may qualify. These plans are often restricted to members of the group with which the society is affiliated. In many ways these plans are very similar to employer provided plans in the way that they interact with Medicare as a Part C component, though of course the best source of information is an administrator of the plan itself.

Qualifying for Medicaid

If your income is low, then there will be other options on the table in the form of Medicaid. Medicaid is a blend of state administered and federally funded programs and as a result, details of the program vary from state to state. To find out more, contact your state Medicaid office.

Where you Live

While the beneficiary's health history or any other personal factors don't affect Medicare Advantage plans, the beneficiary's residence will affect the availability and cost of different plans. In 2013, the average beneficiary was able to choose from about 20 different plans.

Using the Medicare Plan Comparison Tool

Access Medicare's special Medicare Plan Finder at *plancompare.medicare. gov*. Enter your zip code to specify your region, and you'll be on your way. The Medicare Plan Finder tool also allows beneficiaries to enter in all their prescription drugs, so these factors can be taken into account during the tool's analysis. A star-based system ranks different Medicare Advantage plans on the basis of customer satisfaction and the level of quality that each plan offers. Beneficiaries should stick to plans rated 3.5 stars or higher. Plans that are ranked 4 stars or higher receive additional funding from the government to bolster the plan's effectiveness. Another ranking system is available through the National Committee for Quality Assurance.

Medicare Part C vs. Medigap

Medigap (reviewed briefly in Chapter 2) and Medicare Part C are both aimed at picking up the slack for Medicare in certain areas, but how does a beneficiary know which is the most efficient and cost-effective bridge?

There's really no good way to make this determination without evaluating both the Medigap and Medicare Part C plan on an individual basis to find the best fit for the beneficiary's unique needs. While Medigap plans are essentially uniform, they are offered through private insurers and the expenses will vary, so it's important to shop around. Medicare Part C plans, unlike Medigap, will offer different types of coverage and methods for limiting out-of-pocket expenses.

- To review Medigap options in your area, go here: *http://www. medicare.gov/find-a-plan/questions/medigap-home.aspx*

- For Medicare Part C plans, go here: *https://www.medicare.gov/find-a-plan/questions/home.aspx*

You may also want to schedule a time to talk to a Medicare Part C agent or salesperson. Ask one of these agents to help you understand the potential differences in coverage between Medigap and Part C and how they'd likely play out during the course of your lifetime. Just remember that these agents are normally working for one of the Part C providers, so do a little independent research into Medigap options after the meeting. While they are more or less obligated to provide you with direct and unbiased information, just like the doctor and the carpenter, it is a good idea to get a second opinion or examine the facts on your own.

Dental & Vision Coverage

When shopping for Medicare Advantage plans on the *Medicare.gov* website, take note of the small, circled Ds and Vs included in the plan listings. These are indicators that the plan includes dental or vision coverage. There should be a link titled, "View More Detailed Cost and Benefit Information." Click this to learn more about these additional benefits.

Prescription Drug Benefits Through Part C

There are essentially two ways to get a prescription drug benefit plan through Medicare. One way is to use Medicare Part D (discussed in the following chapter). The other way is to choose a Medicare Advantage (Part C) plan with a prescription drug benefit. Sometimes, the latter option is denoted in the literature as (MA-PD).

As with other health insurance services offered through Part C, different plans will have different prescription drug benefits. As was mentioned previously, the Medicare plan finder tool at *plancompare.medicare.gov* will require you to enter in all the prescription drugs that you take and will advise you on a Medicare prescription drug plan accordingly.

A Word of Warning

Medicare Advantage may seem relatively cut and dried based on the facts on the surface: health insurance companies want your money, so they will give you some perks in exchange for higher premiums and some other restrictions. What isn't apparent from the surface is the inherent risk for seniors who use Medicare Advantage. Even if you have found a policy that is a good fit for your needs, your insurer may not see it that way.

Insurers can—without justification or cause, and in some cases without warning—hike up premiums, alter your benefits package, or even drop your policy entirely. These concerns underscore the importance of extensive research if you intend to select a Medicare Advantage plan, including the use of the Medicare plan comparison tool.

CHAPTER SIX

Medicare Benefits – Part D : Prescription Drug Coverage

The four parts of Medicare are:

- *Medicare Part A : Hospital Insurance*
- *Medicare Part B : Medical Insurance*
- *Medicare Part C : Medicare Advantage*
- *Medicare Part D : Prescription Drug Coverage*

Let's review the next part in more detail:

Medicare Part D : Prescription Drug Coverage

Part D is the newest offering in Medicare's insurance suite. Medicare Part D is the prescription drug benefit and is offered alongside original Medicare. If a beneficiary enrolls in a Medicare Advantage plan that comes with its own prescription drug benefit and then enrolls in Medicare Part D, that beneficiary will cease to be covered by the Medicare Advantage program and will from that point forward be covered by original Medicare.

Premiums & Deductibles for Part D Coverage

Premium payments for Part D coverage—like premiums for Medicare Part B—vary with income. If an individual reports an income of $85,000 or less annually, then he or she pays no Part D premium, only the standard Part B premium. If a couple reports an income of $170,000 or less, then they will not pay any premium other than their Part B.

Higher income levels will have an additional amount added to their Part B premiums to pay for their prescription drug benefits. Add-on income-based premiums for Part D range from $12.30 to $70.80 extra per month.

Required deductibles vary depending on which plan is chosen. Some plans have no deductible. No plan may have a deductible greater than $320; that amount will increase to $360 in 2016.

Tiers & Co-payments

Part D plans divide pharmaceuticals into various *tiers* to designate how expensive each drug is. Once a beneficiary's deductible has been met, he or she will be responsible for any co-payment or *coinsurance* amounts required to purchase various medications according to their tiers. For example, drugs on tier A in a Part D plan may require a $15 co-pay, while drugs on tier B may require a $25 co-pay.

Coinsurance is different from a co-payment. With coinsurance, the amount the beneficiary owes, rather than simply a flat amount, is derived as a percentage of the drug's total cost. For example, if a drug costs $200 and requires a coinsurance payment of 20%, then the beneficiary will pay $40 to procure the drug. If that same drug doesn't require coinsurance, but is in a tier that requires a co-payment of $20, then the beneficiary will simply pay $20, regardless of how much the drug costs.

By default, prescriptions are sold and priced on the basis of a one-month supply. Sometimes, however, the beneficiary will not want a one-month supply. For example, if the beneficiary is trying out a new antidepressant with varying clinical effectiveness and heavy side-affects, he won't want to purchase a whole month's supply until he knows for sure that the drug is going to be effective. In order to avoid over-purchasing drugs, beneficiaries may ask their providers to prescribe less than a full month's quantity.

Different Part D Prescription Drug Plans

Unlike Medicare Part A and B, Part D isn't essentially the same plan across the board. Though Medicare funds Part D plans, private insurers administer them. Various Part D plans are available, and each plan can choose which drugs and which classes of drugs to cover. That said, all Part D plans are regulated through the CMS. The best resource for finding a suitable Part D plan is Medicare's plan finder tool—*plancompare.medicare.gov*—which allows beneficiaries to search plans according to their own unique prescription drug needs.

If you'd rather steer clear of the Internet, then you can shop for Part D plans using the Medicare handbook that will be sent to you in the mail (usually in September). You will also receive marketing promotions and information from plan administrators in your area who want you to choose their Part D plans. Another option is to call Medicare at 1-800-633-4227 and have a service representative work with you to narrow down your choices for a good Part D plan. You don't have to choose the plan over the phone, but the representative should be able to send you your detailed short list via email or through regular mail.

Once you choose a Part D plan you will have to stick with it throughout the calendar year, so make sure you exercise good judgment. As your medical priorities change, it's always a good idea to go back to the plan finder (or whatever search method you're using), even after you already have a plan, and take a look at what other, better plans may be available to you. October 15th through December 7th is your open enrollment period. This is the time to make a change if you believe one is necessary.

What if my plan doesn't cover the drug I need?

You have certain rights as a Medicare beneficiary under Part D. One such right is to receive a written ***coverage determination*** from Medicare explaining why your plan won't pay for a certain prescription or won't subsidize a reasonable share of the cost. You also have the right to ask for an ***exception*** which, if granted, will compel your insurer to provide you with the drug you seek. Exceptions must be accompanied by a note from your doctor that gives a medical justification for why the reasons stated in the plan's coverage determination aren't applicable to you.

Perhaps you have already tried the drug that is cited in your coverage determination and it is ineffective, or perhaps you responded to the drug poorly. Or perhaps you have a negative reaction to the drugs on your drug plan's preferred list and the non-preferred drug you need is available only with a very steep co-payment. Applying for an exception may compel the drug plan to reduce the co-payment. Your pharmacist will be able to provide you with a notice explaining how to contact your Medicare drug plan for a coverage determination or an exception decision.

CHAPTER SEVEN
Medicare & Other Insurance Plans

From your employer, to the military, to your union, there is a multitude of institutions out there that offer health insurance. In this chapter we'll explore some of the common interactions, or 'Coordinated Benefits', that arise when multiple insurers are in play.

Let's start with the most common scenario:

Medicaid

There are approximately 65 million Medicaid recipients in the US. One out of five Medicare beneficiaries is *dual eligible*, meaning that he or she also qualifies for Medicaid assistance. Depending on which state you live in, Medicaid may take on a different name. In California, it's called "MediCal." In Massachusetts, it's called "MassHealth." And then there are the majority of states that simply call it Medicaid and it is individual states that are responsible for determining eligibility. For Medicare beneficiaries, being dual eligible makes things a lot simpler and less expensive.

Medicare beneficiaries who also qualify for Medicaid receive an expanded suite of benefits. Custodial care in a nursing home, for example, is available to dual eligible individuals but not to those who only have Medicare. Dual eligible individuals are also eligible for longer paid care in *skilled nursing facilities (SNFs)*. Medicaid pays Medicare's out-of-pocket expenses as well.

For prescription drugs, dual eligible individuals receive low-cost or free prescriptions through a program called Extra Help. For starters, Extra Help completely eliminates the 'doughnut hole' problem, meaning that your drug expenses remain covered without interruption.

The doughnut hole is an endearing sounding term for a potentially damaging financial situation. After a $295 deductible, Medicare Part D is very effective at helping seniors pay for their prescription drugs by taking care of 75% of costs. The problem—the doughnut hole—arises when the cost of those same drugs hits $2,700. After this point the Medicare recipient is responsible for the full cost (100%) of the medication for the next $3,453 worth of doses or refills. After the three and a half thousand dollar threshold is reached, Medicare steps back in to alleviate the costs of medication.

This is a well-known and documented gap in coverage that has, until recently, not been legislated out of the Medicare program. Extra Help is a fantastic program for combating the doughnut hole, but not all seniors qualify. Other ways to reduce the damage of the doughnut hole are to use generic drugs whenever possible (generic drugs are cheaper), and failing that, see if the drug company itself has a payment assistance program.

Under the legislation if the Affordable Care Act some steps have been taken to reduce the financial damage that the doughnut hole can cause. The ACA is covered in greater detail in Chapter 8.

Applying for Extra Help is done through Social Security, not Medicare. Applications can be submitted online at *https://secure.ssa.gov/i1020/start* or by calling the Social Security Administration at 800-772-1213 or TTY 800-325-0778. You can also apply in person at your local Social Security office or State Health Insurance Assistance Program (SHIP) office. You may also apply by mail. Look for the Extra Help application; it should automatically come in the mail from Social Security when you approach age 65.

When you enroll in Medicaid, you will begin receiving your drugs from Medicare Part D coverage rather than from Medicaid. Don't be alarmed. You're still enrolled in Medicaid. You'll get a letter from Medicaid—sent in a purple envelope—to confirm that you are automatically enrolled in Extra Help. If you don't receive the letter, then you should apply for the program.

Some individuals won't qualify for full coverage under Extra Help but will qualify instead for partial coverage. This means they'll receive discounted prices on their prescription drugs, lower than what they'd get under standard Medicare Part D coverage. Even partial coverage through Extra Help will prevent you from having to deal with the doughnut hole.

Other benefits of Extra Help:

- Those qualifying for Extra Help can switch their Part D drug plans whenever they wish rather than having to wait for the open enrollment period.

- Your Extra Help prescription drug coverage will not affect your other benefits1 from SSI, such as food stamps and discounts on heating and cooling.

- Extra Help beneficiaries get free or reduced premiums on their Part D drug plans. The determination as to what, if any, premium you will incur is based on the average premium paid for Part D plans in your region.

If the plan you select has a premium that's less than the average, then you will have it waived entirely. If it's above the average, then you will pay the difference between your Part D plan's regular premium and the average. If you do not choose your own Part D drug plan, then Medicare will select one for you, and it may not be the best fit. If Medicare automatically enrolls you in a Part D plan, then you'll get a letter in the mail (it will be printed on green paper) informing you of your new plan. This is done at random. The good news is that since you're an Extra Help member, you can switch to a different drug plan whenever you want.

> Even if you apply and qualify for Extra Help, you will still need to select and enroll in a Part D drug plan that's a good fit for your needs, so remember to utilize the Part D plan finder tool at—
> *plancompare.medicare.gov.*

Medicaid Medical Spend Down Programs

In some states, Medicaid offers a special program called a "medical spend down" program, which benefits individuals who aren't wealthy but have too much income to qualify for Medicaid. If you qualify for a spend down program (qualification requirements vary from state to state), then Medicaid will provide financial assistance for Medicare expenses, such as co-pays and deductibles, after you spend a certain amount of out of your own pocket.

Spend down programs are nice to have, but unfortunately, most states require that eligibility be continually renewed, often as frequently as every six months. Many individuals find their eligibility in constant flux. This is because once Medicaid begins covering your out-of-pocket expenses, your total health care expenses go down, often making you technically ineligible for the spend down program during the next six-month cycle. This vacillation in eligibility is commonly referred to as "the yo-yo effect".

PACE Programs

PACE stands for Programs of All-Inclusive Care for the Elderly. These programs are supported by a combination of Medicare and Medicaid resources. The objective of PACE is to allow individuals who qualify for nursing home care to receive day-to-day living care in their homes. PACE helps seniors with everyday needs such as meals, transportation, safety, accessibility, dentistry, and counseling.

Unfortunately, the PACE program isn't available everywhere. As of 2014, the program was only operating in 30 states—88 centers all together—and serving approximately 20,000 individuals. To find out if a PACE program is available near you and whether you qualify, contact Medicare at 1-800-MEDICARE (1-800-633-4227), TTY 1-877-486-2048. Or you can check the website: _www.Pace4You.org._

How Medicare Interacts with Your Insurance

If you are covered by one or more health insurers, then you will need to watch closely for a special mailer that you'll receive about three months before your 65th birthday, or three months before you become eligible for Medicare for reasons other than age, such as becoming disabled. In the mailer is a form called the _Medicare Initial Enrollment Questionnaire_. Instructions for filling out this form will be included in the mailer.

Medicare will use the results of your Medicare Initial Enrollment Questionnaire to determine how your claims will be paid if you have one or more additional medical insurers. Medicare makes this determination using a *coordination of benefits* system. This system essentially incorporates Medicare and your other insurers into specific hierarchies to determine which insurer pays for which claim, and how much. The CMS has spent a lot of energy making sure that the coordination of benefits system is well maintained, because, to Medicare, it is an important cost saving device.

The CMS (Centers for Medicare and Medicaid Services) doesn't want Medicare to pay any more than it needs to for its beneficiaries' medical claims, but it does want the claims to be paid in full and on time so that the beneficiaries don't have to worry and micromanage who pays what. This is why filling out the Medicare Initial Enrollment Questionnaire is so important. If you provide all the necessary information about your other insurers, then Medicare will see to it that the proper prioritization is utilized in the discharge of your medical and hospital bills.

The main determination that Medicare needs to make is whether it's going to serve as your primary or secondary insurer. Some of the steps used to make this determination were discussed in Chapter 2 of this book. In general, if you're currently employed and covered by an employer-based insurance plan and your employer employs at least 20 people, then your employer-based insurance will serve as your primary insurance. Otherwise, it will probably be Medicare that is listed as primary.

Things change, of course. For example, if you retired from your job, then your insurance coverage would likely be altered in some way, and Medicare may be your new primary insurer. When your outside insurance is changed in any way, Medicare should be notified. Your contact point for reporting these changes is the Medicare Coordination of Benefits Contractor (COBC). The COBC can be reached by phone at 800-999-1118. The COBC is also your contact point for any questions you have about coordination of coverage.

Employer-Based Insurance & Medicare

Theoretically, your company's (or your spouse's company's) HR department should be able to accurately answer any questions you have about how its insurance interacts with Medicare. Unfortunately, there are some incompetent administrators who may provide bad information. This book has not yet discussed the scenario in which someone qualifies for Medicare before the age of 65 due to disability. If this person has an employer health plan, *and* is still working, *and* is working for a company that employs 100 or more workers, then the employer will probably be the primary insurer. Medicare will be the primary insurer if the employer has fewer than 100 workers.

The reason for the soft language here—usually, generally, probably—is that there are instances in which smaller employers team up to form an insurance group so that they can offer their employees a health insurance product that they'd not be able to offer on their own. When these groups of smaller employers are joined together, a Medicare beneficiary may find himself working for a company that employs fewer than 20 workers but whose insurance will still qualify as the Medicare beneficiary's primary source.

There are laws that require employers who employ 20 or more workers to maintain the same health coverage options for employees 65 or older as they maintain for younger employees. These laws prevent employers from pushing their over-65 employees onto Medicare to save on health care expense. These laws also extend to the employees' spouses. If your spouse is 65 or older, then your employer (of 20 or more workers) is bound by law to provide him or her with the same insurance provided to spouses younger than 65.

Similar legal provisions apply to the coverage of employees with disabilities; employers cannot stop covering a disabled employee just because he qualifies for Medicare. Furthermore, employers may not offer any kind of financial or other incentives to encourage employees to drop their employer-based health care and rely fully on Medicare. Your contact point, in the event you suspect your employer may be violating these laws, is the Equal Employment Opportunities Commission, which can be reached at 1-800-669-4000.

If you feel that your HR administrator is not reliable when it comes to making a clear determination as to whether Medicare is primary or secondary, then get a second opinion from the Medicare Coordination of Benefits Contractor at 800-999-1118.

End Stage Renal Disease

People with ESRD can qualify for Medicare before the age of 65. If these individuals are also enrolled in employer plans, then these plans will continue to be their primary insurers regardless of company size for at least 30 months after the individual enrolls in Medicare. This is a special provision for individuals with ESRD. The 30-month period is known as the coordination period.

For those of you who may not know, ESRD is a permanent failure of a person's kidneys. A person with ESRD cannot live without dialysis or transplant, and the condition is irreversible. There are a variety of sources for ESRD—high blood pressure and diabetes are two of the main culprits. Otherwise, some drug interactions and injuries can cause ESRD, and in some cases individuals are born with the disease.

Even though Medicare is typically for people over the age of 65, in the instance of ESRD or other extreme kidney related illnesses that require transplant procedures, patients who are younger than 65 can qualify for Medicare coverage for 36 months after their procedure. This is good news; the National Kidney Foundation reports that the average cost of the necessary drug regimens that accompany the surgery exceeds $17,000 per year. The 36-month period only applies to patients who are younger than 65;retirees with coverage are still covered indefinitely.

Since this is an exceptional circumstance, be sure to provide your doctor with both your employer insurance card and your Medicare card so that your bills are paid properly. More information on Medicare and ESRD is available on the Medicare website.

Medicare & Employer-Based Retiree Benefits

Your situation is going to be dramatically different if you are receiving health coverage from your own or your spouse's retiree benefits package as opposed to that which would come from an active employer. Medicare will always be your primary insurer, regardless of the size of your former company. Furthermore, some employers can and will force you to get Medicare once you're eligible in order to retain your retiree benefits. Other employers will leave the ball in your court.

The situation for retirees receiving retiree health benefits is not going to be as uniform as that of active employees. There are no laws that dictate what an employer can or can't do, and as byproduct, there is a wide array of different situations in which you could find yourself. Employers who administer retiree benefits have the liberty to get creative with their Medicare-eligible beneficiaries. Some of them will alter your benefits at age 65 so that their programs will cover only your co-pays and deductibles. Some will pay or help you pay your premiums for a Medicare Advantage (Part C) plan. Some will pay for Medigap coverage on your behalf. Some will pay for additional benefits not offered by original Medicare, such as vision or hearing.

To clarify how exactly your retiree plan interacts with Medicare, talk to your employer, benefits administrator, or union representative.

COBRA & Medicare

COBRA is a health insurance option for retirees or people who lose their jobs. Individuals who find themselves suddenly uninsured because their spouse dies without a survivor benefit in place, or because of a divorce or separation, also use it. COBRA has a bad reputation for being expensive, because individuals who get COBRA are getting the same insurance they had with their employers but are forced to pay both their own premiums and the employer's share of their premiums. COBRA coverage will automatically extend to your spouse or to your dependent children.

As it pertains to Medicare, if you are receiving COBRA benefits at the time you become Medicare-eligible, then COBRA benefits will automatically stop. Medicare will be your primary insurer. Your spouse and children, however, will be able to retain their COBRA coverage for the duration of your COBRA eligibility. If you become COBRA-eligible after you've already begun receiving Medicare, then you can purchase COBRA if you want to use it as a supplemental insurer, but will usually find a more cost-effective Medicare supplement in Medigap.

Federal Employee Health Benefits Program & Medicare

If you're a federal employee or a member of a special demographic— such as a Native American or a disabled coal miner—then you've likely had your health insurance needs taken care of by the Federal Employee Health

Benefits program (FEHB). Medicare-eligible individuals covered by FEHB who are still working are in the same boat as those employed and insured by large employers. FEHB will remain their primary source of coverage, and they have the option to delay enrollment in Medicare Part B without penalty (see Chapter 2).

Medicare-eligible retirees who have benefits programs through FEHB will not be forced to sign up for Medicare. They will essentially have the same coverage as they had before retirement. Signing up for Medicare when eligible, however, will make Medicare the beneficiary's primary provider. At this point the beneficiary may drop his FEHB coverage entirely or keep it. Keeping it is not essential but may provide some valuable benefits such as extended coverage while traveling abroad and more coverage on Medical equipment and supplies.

For a complete run down of the benefits of Medicare/FEHB combined coverage, contact the federal Office of Personnel Management at 888-767-6738, or visit their website: *www.opm.gov/healthcare-insurance/healthcare/medicare/medicare-vs-fehb-enrollment/*.

Tricare

Tricare and Tricare for Life (TFL) is a federally procured health insurance program for active duty military, their spouses, their dependents, and military retirees who served at least 20 years. Tricare acts in just the same way as a large employer's health plan. If you're active duty and 65 or older, then Tricare will remain your primary insurer regardless of whether or not you enroll in Medicare. If you want to wait until you retire to enroll in Medicare, then you can do so without worrying about a penalty. You do, however, need to worry about making sure you're enrolled in Part B Medicare coverage before your official retirement date. Failure to do so may result in the loss of your Tricare benefits. If your spouse is turning 65, make sure he or she also enrolls in Part B before your official retirement date.

Tricare For Life (TFL) is available only to military retirees who are 65 years or older and their spouses or dependents. If you take employment elsewhere after retiring from the military, then you may end up with three different sources of health insurance coverage pending as you approach 65:

Medicare, Tricare for Life, and whatever insurance is offered by your new employer. If this is your situation, it's important to know that you *must* enroll in Medicare Part B in order to be eligible for Tricare for Life benefits. Once enrolled, your current employer (if large enough) will be your primary insurer, Medicare will be secondary, and TFL will be the last insurer to pay medical claims.

Tricare beneficiaries who qualify for Medicare on the basis of disability are also permitted to delay enrollment so long as they're on active duty. For retirees, again, the most important thing to remember is that Tricare will automatically switch over to Tricare for Life after you pass the age of 65. But if you are not enrolled in Medicare by that time, then your coverage will lapse. You will not have Tricare, you will not have Tricare for Life, and you will not have Medicare from the first day of the month in which you turn 65 until you enroll in Medicare. Once enrolled in Medicare Part B you will automatically be eligible to receive TFL benefits, but you will be on the hook for any medical care needed during your lapsed coverage. Similarly, if your spouse turns 65 before you do, then your spouse must enroll in Medicare and switch into Tricare For Life.

Tricare For Life is a premium-free supplemental insurance that's considered to be the pinnacle of Medicare supplements. It pays all your out-of-pocket Medicare expenses, premiums, and deductibles when you use a service covered by both Medicare and TFL. Its prescription drug service is better than any Medicare Part D plan, and you're not even required to choose a Part D plan.

More information about Tricare and Tricare for Life can be found at *www.tricare.mil* or by calling 800-538-9552.

CHAPTER EIGHT
Medicare & Affordable Care Act (Obamacare)

AARP officials have been astounded to discover that many seniors still remain in the dark when it comes to how the Affordable Care Act affects Medicare. Due to the highly politicized nature of the Affordable Care Act—often referred to as Obamacare—there has been a lot of misinformation and speculation. Rumors have circulated that the law would force Medicare beneficiaries to find new doctors, purchase more health care to comply with the ACA, and some rumors even hold that the program as a whole is coming to an end as a result of the act.

Thankfully, these rumors are all patently false.

Below are the four most important facts that you need to know as a Medicare beneficiary as it pertains to the Affordable Care Act:

- Medicare coverage will in no way be interrupted during the process of health care reform. Beneficiaries need not shop and enroll in the open marketplace, but may retain their existing health care coverage through Medicare; whether they possess the standard, Part A, Part B original Medicare, or have a Medicare Advantage plan—nothing changes.

- As was mentioned in Chapter 4 of this book, a new assortment of preventive services are now offered through Medicare that don't count against the beneficiary's deductible or require beneficiaries to remit a co-pay. These preventive services include colonoscopy, mammogram, and annual wellness visits with the beneficiary's physician.

- The prescription drug 'doughnut hole'—a period in which a beneficiary may be required to pay a higher share of costs for prescription drugs until the beneficiary spends enough to qualify for catastrophic coverage—will be closed completely by 2020. As of now, beneficiaries inside the doughnut hole who are required to purchase prescriptions will automatically receive a 55% discount at the counter. These discounts will gradually increase until 2020.

- Medicare constitutes "minimum essential coverage" per the mandate of the Affordable Care Act. If you have Medicare, then you will not be subject to any penalties or fines for failing to possess adequate health care coverage.

The CMS also makes the argument that the Affordable Care Act's provisions will introduce more opportunities and resources to help facilitate better coordinated care for Medicare beneficiaries. Though the Affordable Care Act is a massive piece of legislation with provisions that may prove disruptive to various demographics, Medicare beneficiaries come down on the winning end of the new law.

Other Information Regarding the ACA

Signed into law by President Barack Obama on March 23, 2010, The Patient Protection and Affordable Care Act (more commonly referred to as The Affordable Care Act or "Obamacare") has been the subject of intense scrutiny over the last five years with no end in sight. In tandem with the Health Care and Reconciliation Act amendment, the ACA represents the largest total overhaul of the American health care system since Medicaid in 1965.

Designed to lower the number of uninsured individuals, reduce the total costs of health care for the government and individuals, and improve the American health care system overall, the ACA is an ambitious piece of legislation. Though the Supreme Court upheld the constitutionality of the Affordable Care Act in June of 2012, the law continues to be challenged across the country in and out of state and federal courts.

Among the chief impacts of the ACA is the marked reduction of uninsured persons in the United States. The Congressional Budget Office (CBO) had originally projected the ACA to reduce the number of uninsured Americans by 32 million, lowering the total uninsured population of the US to 23 million by 2019. Due to a successful legal challenge regarding the expansion of Medicaid, those original estimates were changed by 3 million people who will remain uninsured.

The drive to expand the number of insured Americans comes from an effort to improve the quality of life for those without insurance and from the desire to combat the number of Americans who file for medical bankruptcy. Medical bankruptcy is currently the leading cause of personal bankruptcy in the US.

Despite the life of the law and the continued efforts of many proponents of the law to dispel rumors, some misconceptions still exist regarding the controversial aspects of the law.

Death Panels

If you are unfamiliar with this popular misconception, you will agree that the name sounds quite scary. The reality is that 'death panels' are a distortion of claims found in initial drafts of the ACA. The first was a stipulation that elderly citizens could be denied coverage based on their age. The second was a clause that essentially allowed the government to determine whether or not an elderly citizen could continue to receive care based on the severity of his or her illness.

Were either of these proposals passed into law, the outrage would be understandably widespread, but neither is present in the current and legal form of the ACA. We do have the IPAB, the Independent Payment Advisory Board—which is the regulatory committee that can make changes to the coverage and benefits portion of Medicare in the interest of cost-savings.

The IPAB has not now, nor will they ever, made a decision to end an individual's life or cease treatment for a person's medical condition.

Exemptions for Congressmen

Many Americans incorrectly believe that members of Congress are exempt from some of the provisions of the Affordable Care Act. This is simply not true. The ACA actually forces members of Congress to obtain health insurance through an exchange or other program instead of using the Federal Employees Health Benefits Program.

Benefits for Illegal Immigrants

There is a common misconception that the Affordable Care Act produces Medicare benefits for undocumented immigrants. This is wholly untrue; a specific provision of the ACA expressly prohibits granting benefits to "unauthorized aliens" (illegal immigrants).

CHAPTER NINE

Proposed Changes to Medicare

With the continual increase in the cost of health care and the retirement of the Baby Boomers, Medicare is faced with the challenge of remaining financially solvent. During the course of Baby Boomer retirement, the number of Medicare beneficiaries will swell from 47.6 million to 78 million. This population shift is also straining the Social Security System to the brink. In this chapter, we'll take a look at the pros and cons of several proposed adjustments to the Medicare system. If you are familiar with the challenges facing the future of Social Security, you may recognize some of the following proposed solutions as similar to the proposals to keep SS financially solvent.

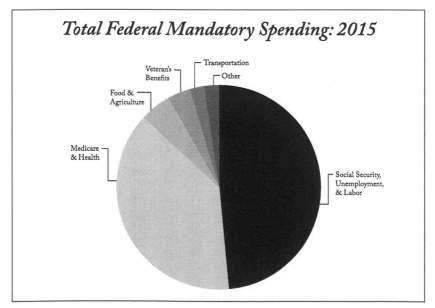

Fg.3 : The total federal mandatory spending for 2015. Source: The National Priorities Project

While Social Security holds the lion's share of mandatory expenditures, the costs of Medicare are rising. Spending in 2015 for Social Security, unemployment, and labor programs was just below half of the government's mandatory budget, ringing in at $1.25 trillion or 48.56%. Medicare, recently expanded under the Affordable Care Act, has grown to 38.4% of that same budget or $985.75 billion[1]. Together, mandatory spending on social programs such as Social Security and Medicare make up far and away the bulk of federal mandatory spending[2].

The current outlook of Medicare is, quite frankly, not so good. Back in 1965 the government's financial planners and forecasting experts predicted that in the year 1990 Medicare would only cost $12 billion adjusted for inflation. Instead it peaked at $107 billion in that year and hit $511 billion in 2009. Needless to say, the program is growing at an alarming pace.

Flat Allocation Funding for Medicare

In this proposal, Medicare beneficiaries would be given a flat amount of government dollars to spend on retirement health care. Private health insurers and the traditional Medicare program would compete for these funds. If an individual wanted to purchase a more comprehensive plan, then he or she could use both the government allotment plus his own out-of-pocket contribution. This plan, as it's currently being proposed, would go into effect only for Americans under 55 years old. Americans anticipating admittance into the traditional Medicare system within the next few years would be unaffected.

This plan would make it really easy for the federal government to control Medicare costs. Once the funds were allocated, it would be up to the individual to decide how to use them. The government would not need to do all the actuarial work and wouldn't incur any risk.

On the downside, the premiums for traditional Medicare would likely climb under this plan, because there would be fewer people enrolled in the traditional Medicare plan. Furthermore, the plan as it's currently being

---

[1] Source: The National Priorities Project

[2] Mandatory spending is differentiated here from discretionary spending, or budgets that change based on need and funds availability such as military spending.

proposed would be inadequately funded. The funding would be based on a market index, which wouldn't truly be able to keep up with the price of health care since health care expenses increase at a faster rate than any other common consumer commodities, which brings us to our next proposed policy change:

Stabilize Health Care Costs

If the cost of health care didn't increase so rapidly, then it would be a heck of a lot easier to keep programs like Medicare financially solvent. But how can the cost of health care be influenced by policy? Here are some of the focal points of the Affordable Care Act's efforts to curb the growth of health care costs:

- **Reorganize incentives so that doctors aren't purely compensated on the basis of how many procedures they perform, but on the ongoing health and wellness of the patients they serve.** These incentives would encourage more attention to preventive care.

- **Ramp up efforts to eliminate fraud and waste in the Medicare system.** All government programs suffer from fraud to some extent. While those who attempt to defraud the government may see it as a victimless crime, the reality is that the misuse and inappropriate use of funds—in addition to being a crime—raises costs for the people the system is meant to help.

- **Reduce the amount of money used to subsidize private insurers offering Medicare Advantage programs.** Doing this would make it a little more difficult for the private companies to compete with original Medicare, but the worst-case scenario would only be that more individuals enroll in original Medicare.

Another initiative that has gained traction since the passage of the ACA is the Independent Payment Advisory Board (IPAB). The IPAB is a group of 15 experts who are in charge of monitoring Medicare expenditures and reducing them when they surpass certain thresholds. In the political arena, the IPAB has become the subject of controversy, being presented by opponents of the

ACA as a 'health care rationing authority'.

Sounds scary, right?

Factually speaking, the IPAB is not permitted to order the reduction of Medicare benefits or the increase in Medicare premiums. It is instead focused on developing incentives for doctors and hospitals to provide more cost-efficient care. In fact, if you're a doctor or a hospital, then the establishment of the IPAB may make you a bit nervous. If health care costs are determined to be rising at a rate that severely outpaces general economic growth, then the IPAB is authorized to cut payments to hospitals, doctors, and Medicare plans, meaning that, though benefits won't decrease, the amount of money doctors make for providing those benefits will decrease. Speaking of paying doctors...

Develop New Ways to Pay Doctors

The current standard used to pay doctors for Medicare services is called Sustainable Growth Rate or SGR. Since its inception in 1997, the SGR has proved unenforceable and ineffective. If the SGR model were enforced today, doctors would automatically receive about 25% less pay.

Nonetheless, there's an undeniable problem surrounding the way in which doctors are compensated, which is essentially on the basis of how many procedures they can squeeze into a working day. The Affordable Care Act introduced incentives to promote better preventive care and ongoing health maintenance, especially for those suffering from chronic conditions such as diabetes. More prevention and fewer procedures means less expensive health care costs across the board.

Raising the Medicare Payroll Tax

Raising taxes is never fun, but it is the most clear-cut and immutable way to increase revenue when it's needed. Currently 2.9% of a person's payroll earnings go to fund Medicare. If employed, the employer pays half (1.45%) and the employee the other half. For persons earning more than $200,000 or couples earning more than $250,000 annually, the amount goes up an extra .9%.

A modest increase (.5% or so) across the board—meaning employees, employers, and the very wealthy all pay half a percent more—could go a long way in stabilizing a system that's on the brink of severe financial hardship in the face of Baby Boomer retirement. That said, increasing taxes is never a welcome course of action; it should be avoided if possible.

Higher Medicare Premiums

It goes without saying: if every Medicare participant put a little more money into the system every month without increasing benefits, then the system would have an easier time staying in the black. The problem with increasing Medicare premiums is that a lot of Medicare beneficiaries are already on fixed incomes and in precarious financial positions. Overburdening them could be problematic, not to mention disruptive to their lives.

Raising the Age of Eligibility for Medicare

One way to reduce Medicare expenditures is to reduce the number of Medicare beneficiaries. Increasing the age of eligibility for Medicare by even a couple years would permanently reduce the quantity of beneficiaries in the system's benefit pool. It would also provide a couple more years for people to pay into the system, as opposed to draw out of it. Furthermore, with the overall increase in life expectancy of Americans, it only makes sense that Medicare and other entitlements should take a little longer to kick in, right?

Well, you've got to consider the opportunity costs. If fewer people were in the Medicare pool, then there'd be more pressure for an increase in premiums. Secondly, if 65 year-olds didn't go straight to Medicare, then they'd still be contributing to expenditures elsewhere in the health care economy, i.e. on their employer's plans or on Medicaid. Furthermore, since the Affordable Care Act subsidizes health care exchanges in the states, who's to say that the cost of subsidizing an exchange plan for the average 65 year-old wouldn't supersede the cost of enrolling that same 65 year-old in Medicare?

Any plans that attempt to index the minimum age to begin receiving benefits to life expectancy (a process called longevity indexing) should be analyzed carefully to ensure that there are no unintentional consequences of such wide-reaching reform.

Changing Co-pays & Deductibles

Another clear-cut way to cut spending on Medicare is to adjust co-pays and deductibles. There are some services such as lab tests that require no co-pay at all from a Medicare beneficiary, even though the same service would normally warrant a co-pay in the general health care marketplace.

Other discussion on Medicare out-of-pocket expenses has focused more so on simplifying benefits. Rather than having a wholly different schedule of co-pays and deductibles for Part A services vs. Part B services, why not have a uniform annual deductible for all health care services?

This organizational streamlining could save money over time. Another idea is to take a page from the Medicare Advantage playbook and have original Medicare plans come with an out-of-pocket limit. Once a beneficiary spends x amount of dollars on co-pays, coinsurance, and deductibles, he or she would no longer need to worry about any other out-of-pocket expenses for the remainder of the year.

Tightening the Belt on Medigap

One factor that drives up health care costs is when beneficiaries visit their physicians unnecessarily or ask for procedures they don't really need. One theoretical way to deter this kind of behavior would be to dilute Medigap coverage or make it more expensive to possess. The supplemental Medigap coverage allows beneficiaries to visit physicians without any co-pay in exchange for paying a higher monthly premium.

Though there's no evidence available to back this up, the theory is that if some co-pay were still required, even by Medigap policy holders, then Medicare beneficiaries would be more discriminating about scheduling doctor visits and requesting procedures.

Negotiate with Drug Companies

One of the less fortunate provisions of President George W. Bush's 2003 prescription drug bill was that it barred Medicare from negotiating with drug companies on prices. Because Medicare is such an enormous consumer of prescription drugs, were it allowed to negotiate with drug companies, it would be able to command much lower prices. The prescription drug bill has been especially hard on Medicaid recipients also enrolled in Medicare. Before the bill, their drugs were procured solely through Medicaid and were subject to price rebates. Since the drug bill went into effect in 2006, Medicaid recipients have been forced to purchase drugs through Medicare Part D, and are no longer able to receive rebates.

To be fair, Medicare's purchasing power, were it allowed to negotiate with drug companies, would cost drug companies billions of dollars, some of which would otherwise be used to spur ongoing efforts to research and develop innovative prescription drugs.

CONCLUSION

Congratulations, after reading this book you are now a big step ahead of your peers on Medicare knowledge. The best way to keep a strong working knowledge on the subject is to keep learning more about it. Re-read this book a few times for starters. Here are some additional resources for you to explore:

Books:

The Politics of Medicare: Second Edition, by Theodore Marmar

If you like learning the old fashioned way, through books, Mr. Marmar's account of Medicare is your go-to resource if you seek a more expansive historical and political reference on the subject.

Online:

Medicare.Gov

The Medicare online base camp—run by the CMS— is a very user-friendly website. It's a little dense with links and information, but the info on Medicare is very much no-frills and to the point, which is nice. The website is also bedecked with nice downloadable PDF pubs that you can read on your e-reader.

AARP.com

The AARP is truly a fount of great information on Medicare; just remember they've got a horse in the race. Through a deal with United Healthcare, the AARP brands its own Medicare Advantage program and they're eager for you to sign up.

National Academy of Elder Law Attorneys

If you or a loved one are suffering from an expensive or complex prolonged illness, the NAELA may be able to help navigate the complicated world of Medicare. The 4,000+ member attorneys specialize in all forms of elder law.

Contact Medicare by dialing 1-800-MEDICARE (1-800-633-4227), TTY 1-877-486-2048.

If you enjoyed the book we would love to receive a positive review from you on the book's product page. Thank you!

GLOSSARY

Advance Beneficiary Notice of Non Coverage -
A notice issued through the doctor's office, or by the provider of equipment or a prescription drug, that informs the Medicare beneficiary that Medicare may deny payment for some or all of the services, products or drugs scheduled to be remitted. This notice must be provided to the patient before these services or products are rendered to the Medicare beneficiary, and the beneficiary will have to sign for receipt of the notice.

Advance Coverage Decision -
Similar to the Advance Beneficiary Notice of Non Coverage, an Advance Coverage Decision comes from a Medicare Advantage plan and provides notice as to whether the plan will cover a particular service.

Assignment -
A medical service provider's agreement to provide services and equipment at the Medicare Approved Amount without billing the patient for more than the coinsurance, copayment, or deductible amount.

Beneficiary -
The recipient of Medicare services.

Benefits -
All services, procedures, products, equipment, and drugs provided by an insurance plan.

Benefit Period -
An allowable period of time during which a Medicare beneficiary may receive inpatient care at a hospital or skilled nursing facility (SNF). The benefit period is used to determine if and how much Medicare pays for these services. The benefit period will expire once the beneficiary has had no inpatient care at a hospital or SNF for 60 straight days.

Centers for Medicare & Medicaid Services (CMS) -
The federal agency in charge of Medicare and Medicaid.

Claim -
A request made to Medicare or another health insurer for payment for medical services.

Coinsurance -
A required percentage payment for the total expense of a particular service. This is separate from a "copay," which is not percentage-based.

Coordination of Benefits -
The process of determining which insurance body is required to pay a claim when the beneficiary has two or more insurance plans that could feasibly be responsible for making the payment.

Copayment or Copay -
A fixed amount to be paid by the beneficiary to supplement the major portion of the expense that is to be paid by the insurer. Unlike coinsurance, copayments are fixed amounts.

Coverage Determination (Part D) -
The decision made by Medicare when determining whether or not, and the extent to which, a certain prescription drug should be covered under your plan. Coverage determinations are usually issued after the beneficiary issues a formal challenge to his drug plan's default coverage schedule. Standard requests must be processed in 72 hours, and expedited requests must be processed within 24 hours.

Coverage Gap -
Also known as "the doughnut hole," a period in which a beneficiary is required to pay a higher share of costs for prescription drugs until the beneficiary spends enough to qualify for catastrophic coverage. The coverage gap begins once the beneficiary has exceeded the amount of initial drug coverage offered by the Part D plan. Coverage doesn't start again until the beneficiary has spent a certain dollar amount as defined by law.

Exception -
When a Part D determination is processed and rendered to allow a beneficiary access to a prescription drug that his drug plan had previously denied or made prohibitively expensive.

Formulary -
A listing of prescription drugs covered by a plan.

Lifetime Reserve Days -
A finite quantity of extra inpatient treatment days that can be used after a Medicare beneficiary has been in the hospital for longer than 90 days during a single benefit period. Original Medicare beneficiaries have 60 lifetime reserve days that can be used during their lifetimes.

Medicaid -
A financially subsidized joint federal-state medical program designed to assist those with very low incomes. Medicaid spills over into the Medicare discussion when assessing special assistance available for those 65 or over with limited incomes.

Medicare -
A robust federal entitlement program signed into law in 1965 with the express purpose of safeguarding the aged population from devastating hospital bills and poor health care conditions.

Medicare Advantage Plan -
Also known as Medicare Part C, or "MA" – Medicare Advantage plans involve contracting private health insurers with Medicare to provide all the same benefits available through Medicare Part A and B. Individuals are attracted to these plans because they can offer expanded coverage for things like hearing, dental, and prescription drug coverage.

Medicare Approved Amount -
A predetermined amount of money that Medicare has agreed to pay its doctors for various services, procedures, products and equipment.

Medigap Policy -
Supplemental Medicare insurance administered by private insurers designed to fill coverage gaps left by original Medicare.

Medigap Open Enrollment Period -
A period in which a new Medicare beneficiary may purchase any Medicap coverage offered in his region and is not limited by any past or present health conditions. The Medigap Open Enrollment Period begins the first month that the beneficiary is covered under Part B.

Original Medicare -
A term used to distinguish between Medicare Advantage options and the standard Part A and Part B coverage that's administered directly by Medicare.

Out-of-Pocket Costs -
Service, equipment, or drugs costs that are at least in-part the responsibility of the beneficiary to pay.

Premium -
The recurring fee required to participate in a health care or drug plan.

Primary Care Doctor -
The principle medical professional who attends to the basic medical needs of a beneficiary. Usually an internist or family practice doctor, the primary care doctor performs basic procedures and tests and refers the patient to appropriate specialists.

Respite Care -
Refers to a temporary period of care given by a nursing home to a beneficiary receiving hospice care, usually administered while the family member or friend who is the patient's ordinary caregiver takes some time off.

Skilled Nursing Facility (SNF) -
A facility with the staff and equipment required to provide semi-complicated and complicated rehabilitative services.

Step Therapy -
A rule used by some Medicare prescription drug plans requiring patients to try one or multiple lower-cost drugs before the plan pays for the more expensive drug that's been prescribed.

Tiers -
Classifications used to organize prescription drugs, usually by expense.

ABOUT CLYDEBANK FINANCE

ClydeBank Finance is a division of the multimedia publishing firm ClydeBank Media LLC. ClydeBank Media's goal is to provide affordable, accessible information to a global market through different forms of media such as eBooks, paperback books and audio books. Company divisions are based on subject matter, each consisting of a dedicated team of researchers, writers, editors and designers.

The Finance division of ClydeBank Media is composed of contributors who are experts in their given disciplines. Contributors originate from diverse areas of the world to guarantee the presented information fosters a global perspective.

Contributors have multiple years of experience in successfully starting and operating online and offline businesses, marketing and sales, economics, management methodology and systems, business consulting, manufacturing efficiency and many other areas of discipline.

For more information, please visit us at :
www.clydebankmedia.com
or contact us at :
info@clydebankmedia.com

GET A FREE CLYDEBANK MEDIA AUDIOBOOK + 30 DAY FREE TRIAL TO AUDIBLE.COM

GET TITLES LIKE THIS ABSOLUTELY FREE:

- *Business Plan Writing Guide*
- *ITIL for Beginners*
- *Stock Options for Beginners*
- *Scrum Quickstart Guide*
- *Project Management for Beginners*
- *3D Printing Business*

- *LLC Quickstart Guide*
- *Lean Six Sigma Quickstart Guide*
- *Growing Marijuana for Beginners*
- *Social Security Simplified*
- *Medicare Simplified*
- *and more!*

TO SIGN UP & GET YOUR FREE AUDIOBOOK, VISIT:
www.clydebankmedia.com/audible-trial

RATTAN - Amazon - Ebike

Made in the USA
Lexington, KY
03 December 2015